Who Lives on

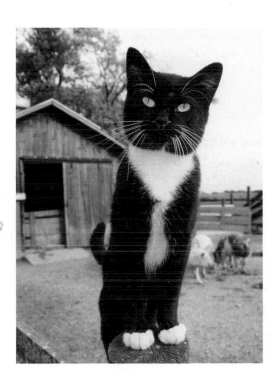

written by Pam Holden

1

We see cows on a farm.

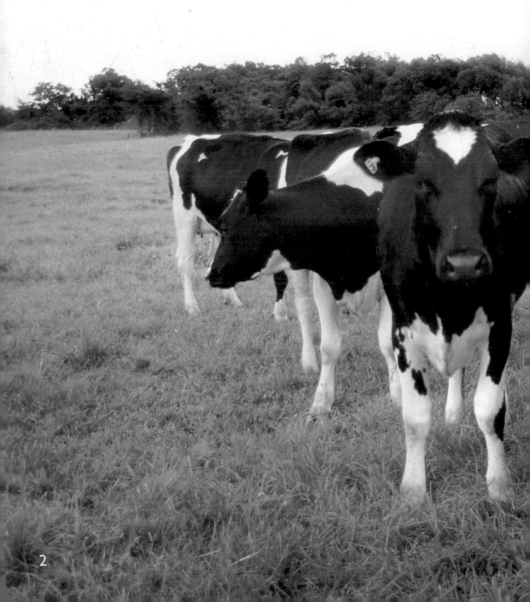

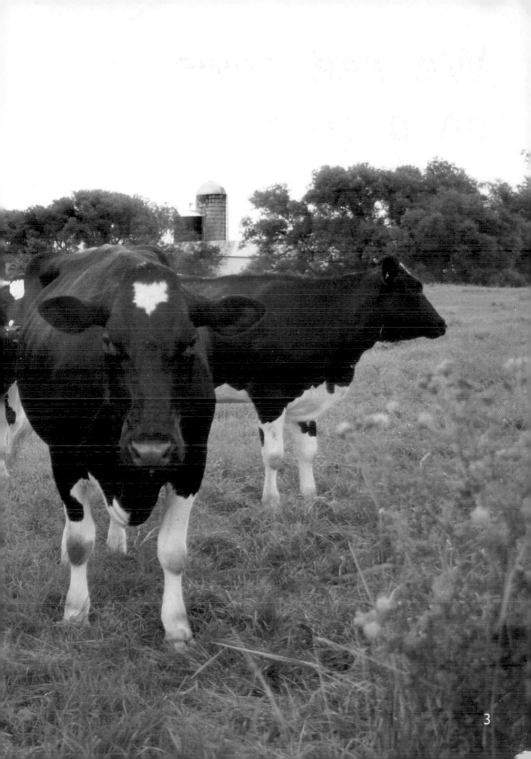

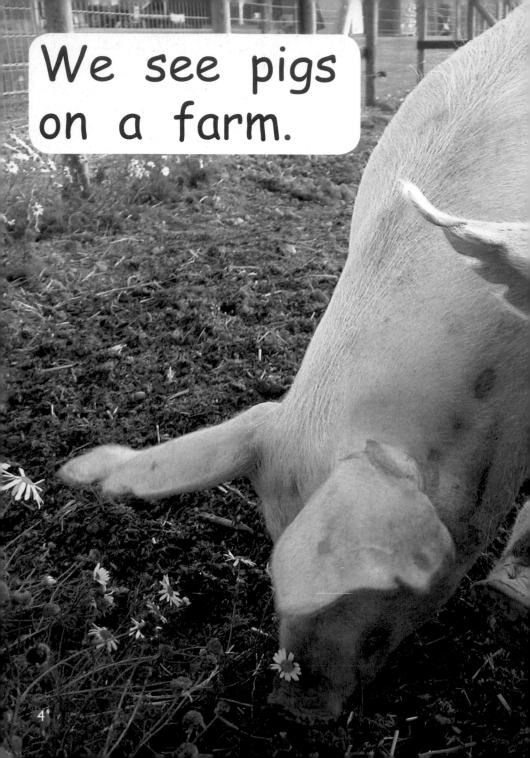

We see pigs on a farm.

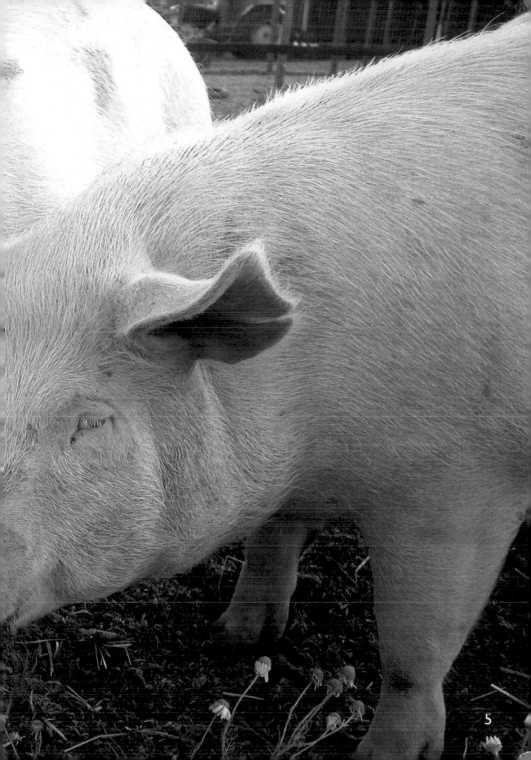

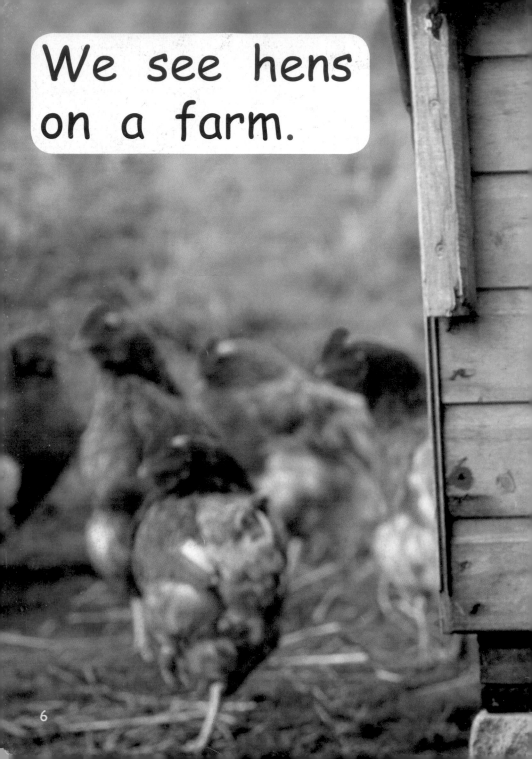

We see hens on a farm.

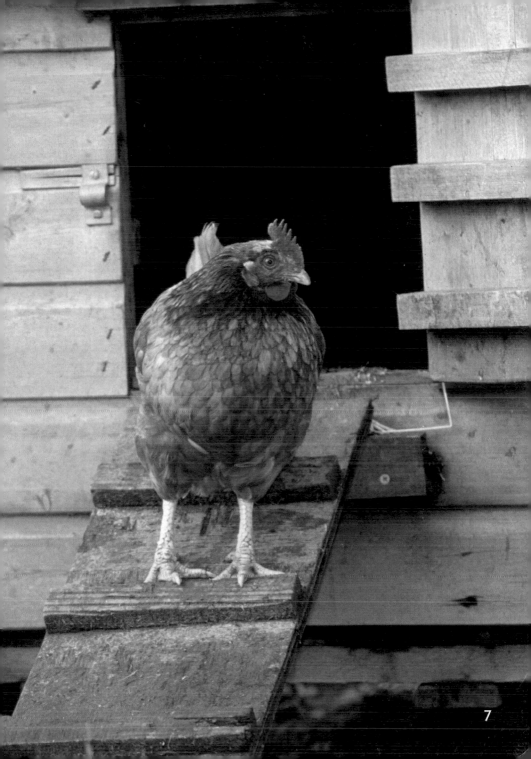

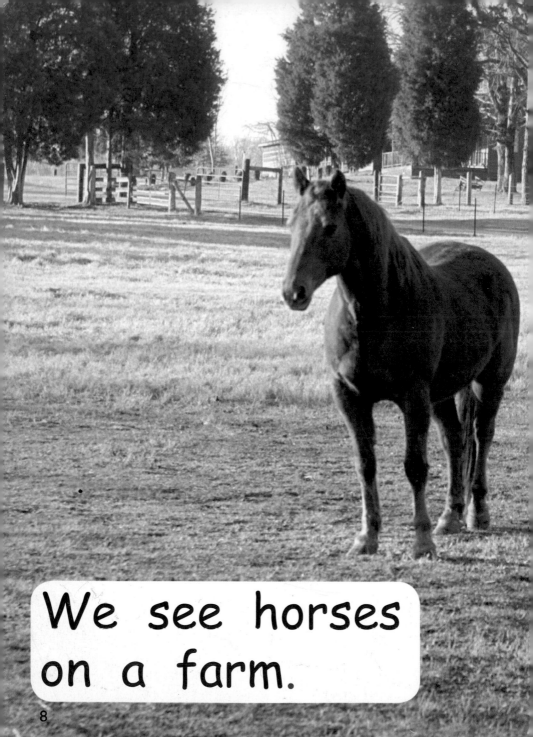

We see horses
on a farm.

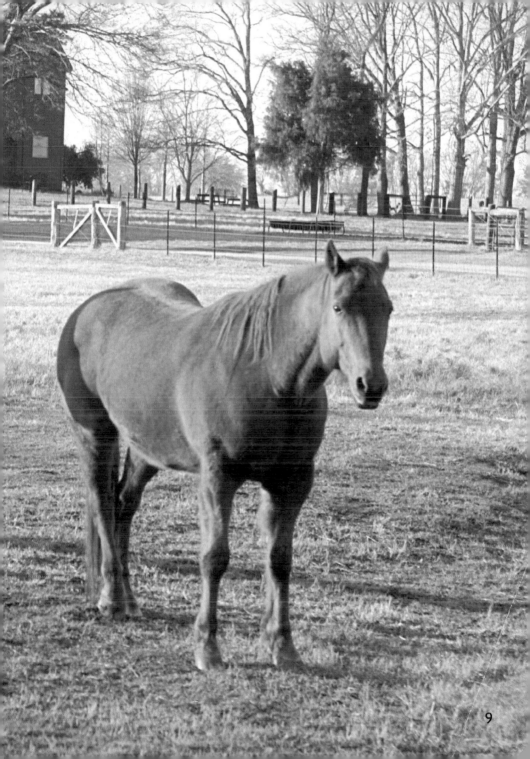

We see sheep on a farm.

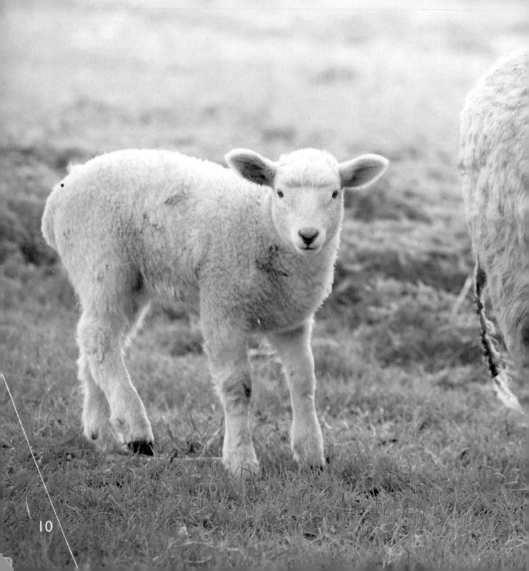

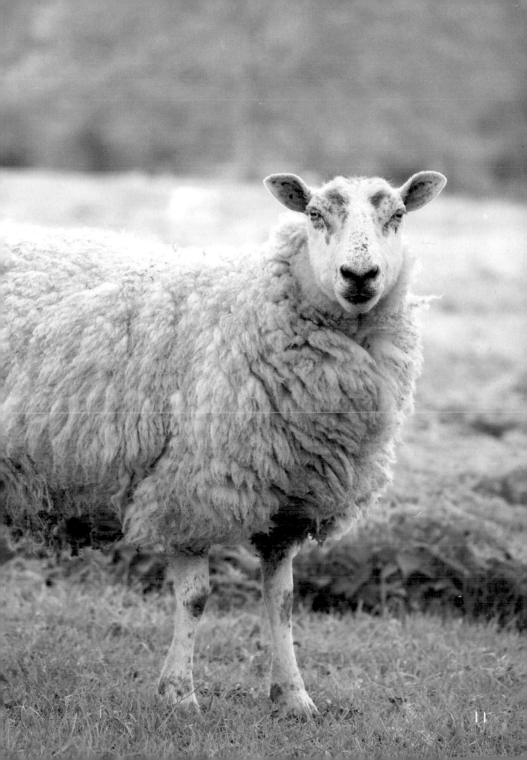

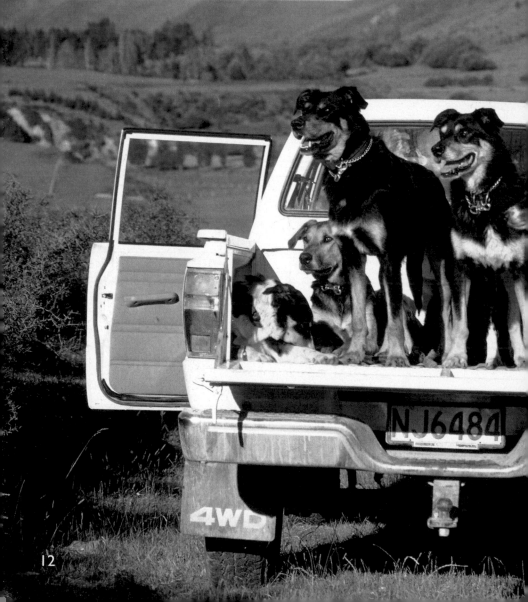

We see dogs on a farm.

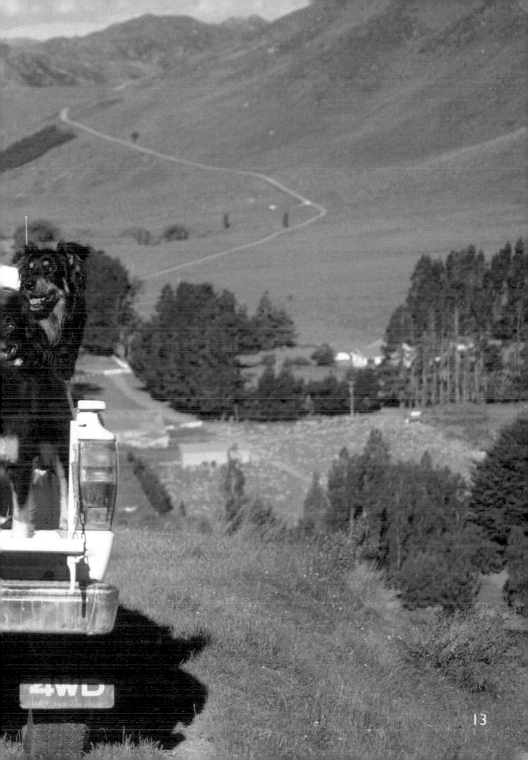

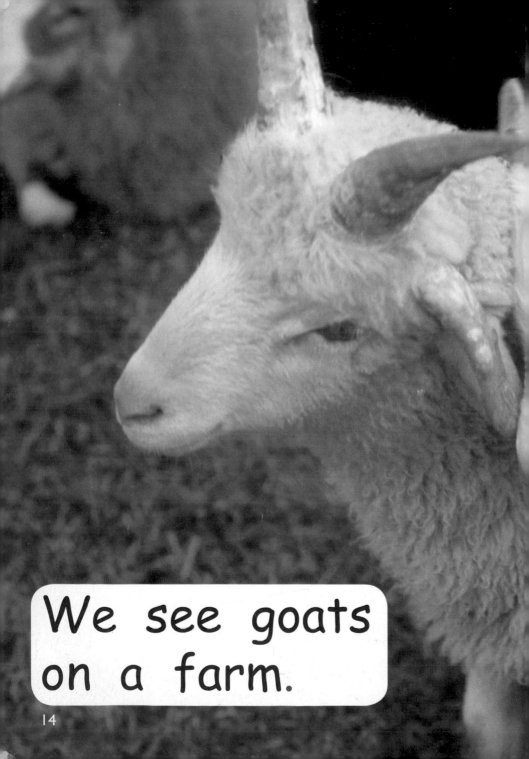

We see goats
on a farm.

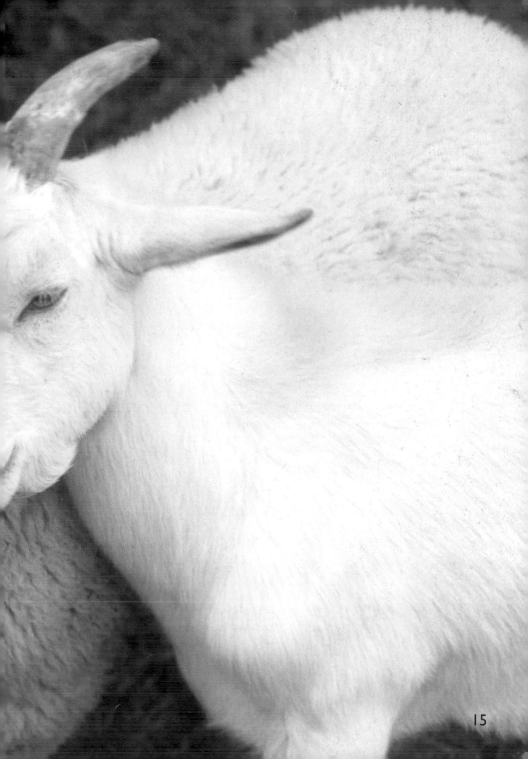

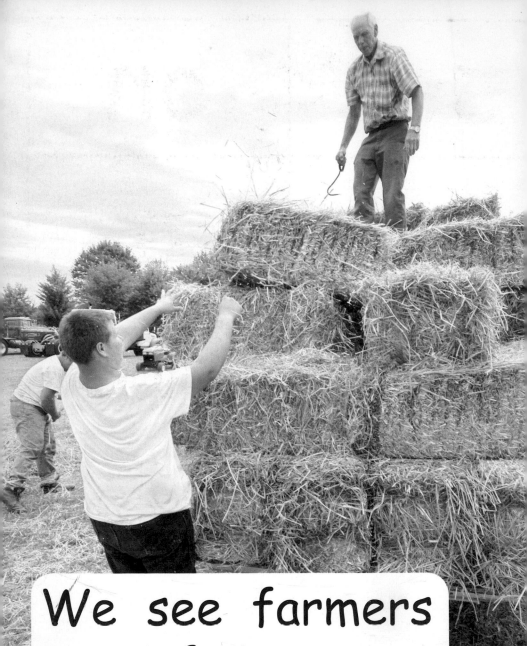

We see farmers on a farm.